MIKE H~~A~~

into a working-class ~~~~~~~~~~~~~~~~~~~ny. He ~~~~~~~~~~
a stand-up comedian, playwright, poet, broadcaster and
documentary maker.

His father was killed returning from a bombing mission just
four weeks before Mike was born. This had a profound effect
on his childhood and later life, and much of the inspiration for
his writing comes from his early years growing up in Manchester.

His writing has ranged from comedy to church architecture,
from poetry to playwriting, from short stories to novels and,
unsurprisingly, from fell-walking to a manual for fishermen on
how to tie flies, with many of the books illustrated with his
own photographs.

Luath Press has also published Mike's poetry collections
Connemara Cantos and *Strange Lights Over Bexleyheath*. He
has recently completed a new play about a bombing raid over
Germany in the last war, inspired by childhood memories of his
father's death.

Although born and raised in Manchester, Mike's lived in the
Yorkshire Dales for the past 40 years – a lot longer than he
lived in Lancashire. The move – in 1971 – was prompted by his
love of fell-walking, fly fishing and the countryside in general.

With the Dales as his base, Mike walked and cycled,
photographed and lived among the farming community. He
became President of The Ramblers for a three-year term and is
now a lifetime Vice-President. He is in constant demand to
speak on environmental and ecological issues and has been
elected a Fellow of the Royal Geographical Society.

And he's even been known to admit that there are times
when he wishes he'd been born a Yorkshireman.

Fishing for Ghosts

MIKE HARDING

Luath Press Limited
EDINBURGH
www.luath.co.uk

First published 2017

ISBN: 978-1-910745-85-4

The paper used in this book is recyclable. It is made from
low chlorine pulps produced in a low energy, low emissions manner
from renewable forests.

Printed and bound by
Bell & Bain Ltd., Glasgow

Typeset in 11.5 point Sabon
by 3btype.com

Contents

Introduction

The poems here were written mostly over the last three years. All came by accident. I never sit down with a blank sheet and think, 'Now I must write something.' That never works for me.

A phrase, an image, an unbidden thought, and the notebook that is always in my pocket is opened again. Some of the poems went down on the page almost whole, almost fully fledged and ready to fly, others came piecemeal and were nudged and whittled or hammered until it seemed that they would live; the ones that didn't open their eyes and shout are in the drawer waiting in the dark.

Some of the poems in these pages are love poems in so far as that is what inspired them – love of a land or people rather than a person; some were born of anger and for that I make no excuse. There is an old Chinese curse, 'May you live in interesting times.' We live in interesting times and for a poet not to speak out, to stare fixedly at his or her navel as the building burns down and the fat cats scamper off with their booty would be an act of treachery.

Acknowledgements

The cover image is the work of a very talented Croatian photographer, Robert Gojević, who is both an artist and alchemist. As a child, I was fascinated by the work of the Zagreb school of glass painters like Ivan Generalic and it is ironic that so many years later I came across an artist from the same region who works with wet silver salts on glass. I stumbled on the picture completely by accident. Robert calls it Sea Ghosts and I thank him for permission to use it here.

The Snow Goose

We loved it when the great Snow Goose
Let loose her moon-dust feathers, the soft down flocking
All about the shrieking, school-free town. Loose
Wellies flapping, mittens made from stockings

On our little hands, heads in balaclavas.
In the yards the great snowmen stood guard as
In the street the tin-tray sleighs went skittering over cobbles
Sunk beneath an inch of ice. You hobbled

Round, your socks worked down
For ice bees and chilblain imps to bite. You played
Out late, in that bone-white world, afraid
Of the Snow Queen and her evil splinters. Stayed

Alone watching the gas lamps flutter on
With more goose feathers dancing round their iron arms;
A solitary child in a muted world – a giant had taken
The whole Earth like a great glass ball, shaken

It and put it on the shelf of night
To watch the snowflakes fall. You were so small.
Later you stood quaking, shaking, winter white,
Before the coal fire on the old rag rug, aching

Heels and fingers. And outside the snow goose shed
More feathers, and the great fat snowman in your dad's old shirt
And carrot nose, smiled as though his snowball head
Under the flickering lamp, held all the secrets of the universe.

Cissy Worswick Waltzes

My first teacher, you seemed so very old;
Your hair up in a tight French roll, your gold
Rimmed glasses flashing, your thin, long,
Chalky fingers and your icy, lashing tongue.
I feared you then Miss Worswick, feared your bony clutch,
Your slap, your razor voice, I feared you very much.

And yet, long after you were dead, I met in church
A woman who had known you in those times.
She told me how you spinstered round the house
Skivvying for aging parents – daughter, slave;
No time for dancing or for walking out,
Your job: to serve them on their journey to the grave.

And yet, you said after the Sunday roast, each week
When they were upstairs taking their after dinner sleep,
You used to close the curtains, pour yourself a sherry
And strip stark naked in the damask dark. Merry

And electric with the wine you waltzed about the house
Feeling, you told your old friend, 'Somehow
Deliciously wicked.' In this small, pure innocent way
You found your sole delight in those cold, chain-child days.

So dance, Miss Worswick dance, all naked round the room,
Let the soft light spilling through the gaps hold you like a
     groom,
Let warm summer shadows waltz you faster, faster,
Past the aspidistra, brass coal scuttle, antimacassars.

Another glass of sherry, Cissy, let it warm
You like the sun whose golden tongue

Creeps through a sliver of curtain crack,
As you dance to your whispered song,
Searching the old maid Sunday gloom,
To kiss your unkissed breasts, your soft downed back.
As on and on you sashay round the summer-dark room.

Dance until the stars come out, Miss Worswick,
Dance until the Salford cobbles bloom,
Or until the shuffling footsteps on the boards above
Tells you that it's time to dress again, to banish dreams of love,
To let the dying evening light in from the summer street,
To set three places out and scald the pot for tea.

Back of the Drawer

Rooting about, a child, your little fingers
Digging amongst the jumble in a drawer,
A little archeologist turning the soil,
You find old forks with broken tines
And yellowed ivory handles,
A broken cameo, a lace doily,
A scatter of half-spent birthday candles,
A box of buttons and a watch that hasn't gone
In years, a catechism, a jet necklace,
Three odd cufflinks, and an empty purse;
At the back, a yoyo with no string, and further in
A tarnished brass star in a treacle toffee tin.

You take it out and hold it up
And when you ask, he turns, 'Oh that.'
He says, 'That's nowt. Put it away.'
And back away it goes. Six years
Abroad, his thanks: a ribbon and 'a gong'.
The rest of his platoon now lies along
The Burma Railway. In that small tin box are blood
And fear and ghosts in ragged shorts with bleached
Twig legs and screaming skulls; his war.
In that small tin is 'nowt.' You close the drawer.

Trainspotting

Victoria Station Manchester 1954

A black snake moan, a great blue hiss
And then the pistons slug it out. 'Bouff!!'
A massive breath out as the blow hits home
And the boxer punches hard enough to send
The iron wheels slip-skittering on the steel.
And then it grips, and then it tortuously
Starts to slowly roll, dribbling like
A shrugging waking beast, Samson in harness.

The piston's sleek oiled rods seem far too slim
For that wild elemental force,
Steel, iron and fire and brass, the ramrod thrust
And push, the boiler's belly
Tended by the sweating, fire-glazed men.
We sense not engineering, slide rule, castings, lathe,
But some mad creature, some black behemoth,
Struggling, into the day unchained.

And then it gathers speed a little, barks
And coughs, triumphant, thick, coal smoke and steam
That shrouds the glassy roof. It belches, sparks
And heaves its long black body hunched
And urgent in a slow beginning;
Gathering now and grunting now
And lunging now and hunting now
And urgent now and panting now,
And shouting now, and boastful now;
Dragging it's clanking, grumbling
Train of jumbled carriages from out

The giant cavern with its soot
And steam, glass roof and iron tree boles, out
Into the sudden summer light of somewhere else.

It leaves behind a cloud of pigeons
And a flock of school-free boys
Chasing it until the final yard of lined platform,
Watching its dragon's tail snake out beyond the city's edge,
Standing in the sun to write its name
And number in their sixpenny books
As it sashays off, an ignorant great brute,
Away into a brightness of far horizons
Across a burnished sea of silver rails.

The Long Goodbye

Was it two years ago or three the names began to fade
Like yellowed snapshots left out in the sun,
Or footprints in the sand, as one by one,
They went, scoured by the relentless tidewash of the days?
The words fall from the images,
Dried labels peeling in a family album,
And we recede into the future
As you grapple for our names.

Was it around the time you left
The gas ring on all night,
Put letters in the fridge,
And thought the Spring sunlight
Reflected on the ceiling was a dapple of
Small birds sent here for your delight?
And you lay back, your mouth agape,
Hands waving, eyes child-bright
Smiling at the swirl of birds,
Like a six-month baby in a pram
Delirious with its new found world.
Was it last year when you dug down for words
Like 'radiator,' 'newspaper,' 'belong,'
And found no treasures only broken shards,
Lacunae, fragments, clay tablets in another tongue?

Now you are a wireless tuning in at random to a host
Of strange lost worlds and you re-broadcast news,
Snips of drama, weather forecasts, arcane spells.
Day follows day in this tortuous farewell,
As you turn from that face-wiping, sock-darning,
Late-chiding, bruise-soothing mother of years past
Into a tabernacle of dry sticks and paper skin,

A cage of bone from which the singing bird has gone,
A Chinese lantern with a guttering flame –
Some days you do not even know my name.

Time shows no mercy, and the planets spin,
The stars turn and we shuffle endlessly towards
That beach and that all-encompassing sea.

And there you lie, our mother the kite,
All sticks and skin, breath-light,
Waving at the ceiling flock of birds
With your rattle-bone hands and goodbye eyes,
Waiting for the winds of this wide world
To carry you away into the endless skies.

Pan Pipes – Durham – 2014

An unexpected, brass-bright late November day
A day of clear sky, sun and port-wine warm;
This Saturday square is speckled with a swarm
Of children, OAPs and shoppers; all hearts lift
Souls lightened being somehow gifted
With this summer-in-winter day.

A jumble of small kids jig to a busking band;
A swirl, a hoom of Andean pipes,
The throb and boom of drums,
The rattle of the rainstick and the lads
In denims, condor feathers and Ray Bans
Bring ice capped mountains and La Paz to northern streets.
And then one swirl of notes, a slither up the scale,
Is suddenly a key that opens up for me
The rummage box of the forgotten years,
And I take out the summer I was six.

You bought me plastic panpipes from
The market, and from sun to dark
Those golden days I walked about
The burning streets weaving my music
In the humming air, free to wander anywhere;
I was tied still fast to your apron strings
By a whirligig of notes. You found me by just winding in
The skein of windsong, owlsong fluting,
Following as it led you through the streets to me.

The pipes they echo all around the square
And I expect you any moment to appear
Dusting floury hands, curlers in your hair
Blinking in the sun and saying, 'So – you are there!'

Ward F3

'And what are all these people doing in my home?'
She asks, her twig hands on the counterpane
Kneading the linen like a kitten at the teat;
Her breath-light body shaking in
The barbarous high winds of the years.
'Mum, it's a hospital.' I say, the words
Take to the air like heavy birds
Circling for a roost. 'It's not my house?'
'No it's the hospital. You've been poorly.
You're ok now.' 'Can I go home?' she asks,
Her false teeth clacking in her shrunken gums.
'The doctors say you can go home quite soon
They're waiting for the medicine to work.'
This is a scene I know we will play out
Each time I come until the end,
A sixty-five-year-old man still calling her
'My mum.' Surely there ought to be
Some other word once we are of an age?

'But what are all these people doing in the house?'
It's not our house mum, it's the hospital
Dad used to work here, you remember – Lou.'
This is her husband, father of three children.

Some lost librarian cell trawls through the archive of
Her mind and finds a broken shelf with 'K' and 'M'
Still there but not the 'Ls.' There is
A long still silence as she thinks; an ambulance
Howls up the snaking hospital drive,
A nurse brings a fresh jug of water to her bed
Takes the dead flowers from the vase

And drops them in the bedside bin.
'It's a very common name is Lou.' She says,
Dwarfed by the bed and smiling at the Filipino nurse
Content, as though with that she has just solved
All the secret, sacred doctrines of the universe.

Today

This is what you will do today:
Today you will eat your breakfast and write home,
You will cycle to the village for some stamps.
You will post the letter, buy some mints,
And you will cycle slowly back to camp.
There are more birds singing here today
You think than you have ever heard;
England has never looked so lovely or at peace.
You take your time, no rush, ops late tonight;
The sentry will cadge a smoke, you will park your bike.
You will check the weather, there will be
A Bombers' Moon, cloudless, a possibility of fog
On your return. You will check your log.

Today you will collect your kit, your chute, your codes;
You will be briefed, and still today,
Once the sun has sunk into the West,
You will take off into the dark night sky; the flatland moon
Bloated and ruddy like a Lord Mayors face rising ahead.

Today you will fly out across the murderous North Sea,
And tomorrow, after midnight, for an hour or two
You will dance upon a floor of flak a mile above the earth.
You will see the burning boys fall wingless from the sky,
And far below, tomorrow, you will see
The jeweled earth clustered with fires
A spattering of rubies, carnelian, sapphire.
Tomorrow you will see all that, before you also fall
Out there beyond salt marshes and the last of land.

But this is what you will do today:
You will cycle with your mints and stamps
The warm sweet country miles to camp;
The hedges clotted with the May, the birds
Will sing, the gears will tick, the chain will whirr;
The fields of England will spread out, away,
Far as the eye can see to the horizon's blur,
Until you reach the airbase – today.

Our Invisible Uncle

An email from my sister, breaking off
From tending our old family tree,
Tells me we have, or had, an Uncle John
Unheard of till she found the link today.
Born in the workhouse, last one of the litter,
And given up, the unwanted pup or kitten.
Recorded only as 'Adopted' in the file.
'Father unknown' nothing relevant,
A copy of his birth certificate – then nothing;
Lost John, long gone is now a ghost, a revenant.

Our grandmother, big bellied, swollen feet
Carried you nine months; fell in the street,
Was taken in on the Parish. Taken in?
'Taken in sin.' They would have said,
'Well girl, you made your bed
Now lie in it.' And there were tuts
And clicking tongues no doubt –
Some doctor or midwife called out
And ten days later she was on her way again.

The baby stares up at the high, tiled walls
Hearing the corporation echoes fall;
In the starched and cold, carbolic room,
The muted and official sounds of civic love.
He's waiting for a nurse to come,
His workhouse bassinet a boat
In which he'll soon set sail,
A little Moses born to glide
Carrying his short life's tale
Between bullrushes at the riverside,
His vessel unseen by the Pharaoh's daughter,
Following the choppy rushing waters
Out into the world of fable and myth.
Your story now lost in Time's mist
But for the fragment here stumbled across.
How far did you go journeying on
Into the love of strangers, our lost,
Our invisible, Uncle John?

The Fire Raisers

Genesis

A shilling plastic magnifying glass
Bought from the paper shop with Saturday spends,
Then off into the dumps we ran, past
Watchmen's huts and on round bends
To where no one would see us. Then
We'd hunker, secret, down and gather
Tinder: bone-dry grass like giant's hair;
And bark, sloughed skin from dinosaurs.
And we would take the glass
And make a burning needle spot,
Willing the grass and leaves to catch.
Kneeling, breath held we watched the hot
Come magic: fire without a match.

Leviticus

A worm of smoke, a dull red eye,
The edges of a bloody wound and then
A long dead leaf would glow, would burst into
A life more terrible, and we would blow
Would nurture, coax the beast, feeding
Its tongues with fescue and dried stalks,
Watching it grow and slobber
Slaver and snap, howling for more.
And so we fed it 'till it weaned itself
Found its own strong legs and tottered off
To find its own food in the heath and grass.
But then it beat its breast, leaped fences, walls
And learned to fly, before our amazed eyes
Became a great fire dragon ranging on the hills.

Revelation

And then we really saw the monster we had made;
Ten heads of flame, and each with seven horns,
Spewing, flocking devil sparks, it's breath
Dimming the sun. Slouching, roaring,
New born, apocalyptic, its hour finally come.
It was gobbling up our whole known world.
And we ran screaming for our homes
Pandoras in short pants and plaits,
Not knowing if our beast would die and fall,
Or grow and grow until it took us all.

The Geometry of Death

In his aluminium eyrie so far above the earth,
That he could touch the stars, as the engines rock his perch,
He plots the bomber's course: arcs, air speed, vectors;
Mapping the Dance of Death towards the chosen sector.

All that Trig and Geometry stands him in good stead,
For he is a navigator, one of the very best.
Yet as his pencil rules its crisp trajectory
Leading to a river, ironworks and factories,

He thinks about that simple graphite line and how
Just one degree, or less – a minute out –
And the fat seed-pods of death, just feet away,
Will spill from out the Lancs' bomb bay

On innocent streets. He sits, an ersatz god,
In his flying kit as the shuddering bird
Roars through the night, one of a flock
Of Lancasters. Time ticking, lines lead on.

They feel their way along the midnight coast,
Following the lines as he plots out
A future he has lost. Flack so thick that you could dance on it
Flies up around the city. He feels a growing pity

As ape-like in his sheepskin coat he rules
His paper world. A bomber's moon above,
Below the city waits, the banshee sirens wail,
Howl out across the sleeping streets.

The scalenes of the searchlights scratch
And score the sky, seeking to catch
And cusp the plane in a cats' cradle of death.
And still the Cumberland graphite, HB, deftly
Rules the lines, lines over lines,
Train tracks, canals and docks;
And still he scribes. But then lines meet
The searchlights intersect and
For a moment holds them in a cone,
Offered like a chalice in the mass.

Night fighters slide in underneath
A line of canon shells and Geometry, the vertex of fate
Has them falling all ablaze, in a perfect chord
Dictated by the plane's air speed,
The wind, the planes weight
And the exact time at which shells hit the wing.
A good man who knew calculus,
With a slide rule and the facts – it wouldn't be hard –
Could tell you where they'd come down, to within a yard.

Returning

So they came home like Ulysses to Ithaca,
Bringing what was left of them back from war
Down half-forgotten streets they had been fighting for;
Some as the evening shadows fell,
Some to the orisons of welcoming bells,
Some to Woodbines, kisses and brown ale;
Some long after the bunting and the flags had paled.

Shot up, wounded, scarred inside and out,
They came back to a world familiar in a way,
But veiled too, a land one step removed
That hardly understood them, or them they.

Back as though they'd just been out the door
For a smoke or nipped across the road
For a gill of mild, a loaf of bread;
Like old men returning, as men always do,
Either in their minds or on their feet
To those far off lands of lost childhood,
They came again. But these are not old men.

Rip Van Winkles, ghosts in demob suits,
Back on the streets again, thinner
Browner and with war-dimmed eyes.
And how does Burma seem in Blackley
Now you're back there in the in the space you left,
In the factory, shoveling dye,
Clocking on each morning at the ICI?

The Desert Rat next door, nerves torn,
Has visions of burnt boys roasted in tanks,
Half in half out, grinning in a rictus at a wadi
That is not comical at all. He has foul dreams.
Kicks, screams, wakes. In the factory he takes
A spanner to the guide that sorts
The custard tarts and Eccles cakes,
But the djebel's never all that far away.

That postman daily walks the streets,
Still with that slight roll that the waves
And the minesweeper gave him.
He puts the letters through the doors
And sees the dead bobbing like khaki seals,
The landing craft ashore, men falling in the sand
As though to sleep, suddenly grown tired.

This bus conductor piloted his crew,
His six blood brothers back from twenty raids,
All safe, all blessed, the flak took other paths
The Schräge Musik played to other ears.
He turns the wheel and Dresden burns
Lighting his way through all the years
Between the dipping of the clutch
And the changing of the gears.

A few pints, some talk of nothing else;
Some never talk of it at all, turn off
The telly when another story of the war
With Hollywood khaki heroes hits the screen.
Six years of madness, six years on the edge,
Six years away – and coming back
Is not even a dream, far more,
A shift in the whole earth. They say,
'What happened out there stays out there.'
But out there is a place they visit every day.

Fishing for Ghosts

I hadn't meant to cast my line for them,
Fishing instead the sea of buried days for dates,
House numbers, who lived where and when –
But not the dead, no not the drowned
Held in the long slow undertow of Time.
I was seeking only facts to pin the story down;
To fix it, filling in my memory's gaps;
A trade directory, census, city maps;
A chart to see me through the maze,
A template for the stories of my days.

But as I reeled the line back in I saw
Holding the cast, eyes fixed on me,
A woman with her hand outstretched.
She came smiling ashore through the slack tide
Hutched on her hip a laughing child.
Then close behind her came a man
In uniform bright medals and a smile;
And clutching to his coat another child,
And then came other figures in groups and alone
And all of them yet somehow looking quite at home;
A great sea web, all holding hands,
Skirt tails, apron strings, waist bands.

A bright young girl with copper hair
Comes dancing through the spindrift foam,
Whispers of light going solid as she stands
And laughs; she's coming hand in hand
With another girl who shakes the sea off
Like a cloak in showers of amber rain.
And they too lead a younger child who holds
A smaller toddler's hand, and more and more
Come gently through the tide's edge to the shore
All smiling, all amused perhaps to be here now?

All linked the lights and stories fill this bay,
Until at last the sea lets up its catch and there I stand
Agog, watching the smiling ghosts of all the days
Talking and walking on the all forgiving strand.

An English Catholic Pastoral, 1958

High summer's day, the best of times, warm, clear
A lapiz sky, late afternoon. The sounds ring out
That made an empire once: leather on willow, cheers,
Boys' voices. Swifts scythe the sky – a shout,

'Howzat!' The umpire shakes his head.
Boys in white flannels fleck the field,
The keeper hunches down, the captain
Waves his fielders further out. Again

The red-haired boy, his belt the old school tie,
Runs up to bowl; a yorker arcs, a crack;
Bails skitter, stumps cant awry.
The batsman grins, shrugs, head high, walks back,

Through sportsmanlike applause that long, hard mile
To the green Edwardian pavilion that smells
Of two-stroke, cut grass, kit and boys and Hell.
Clapping him back in, the lingering monsignor smiles;

Lizard eyes, a smoker's peppermint breath,
The soft pink hands, still clapping; all the power
Granted by the Glory and the spider web.
He waits until the boy comes from the shower.

Later, the groundsman, outfield on his mower,
Sees the priest's black Rover, thought that he had gone.
There are hurried movements in the car, the game is over
Boys cheer, one is weeping, and the stumps are drawn.

The Heart of the Iceberg

'Come in,' he said, and the great mahogany door
Of the web slid open with a heavy hiss
On smooth brass hinges, paneled,
Ponderous as a nightmare. Oh those nuns
Kept it well burnished and well oiled.
Silent sisters with soft cloths
They fluttered along the walls,
Saying little, seeing much those hushed and holy moths –
What wise and silent monkeys they were all.

Outside in its dying hours, the late September sun
Spun buttery bars of fading light along the long,
Cool corridor, dark with the smell of flowers
And beeswax, terror and righteousness.

Introibo ad altare Dei,
The small boy took his child's pure soul
Into the cold, foul night
At the heart of the iceberg
Where the spider in the soutane
And the cummerbund lay in wait.

And still the nuns polished and cleaned,
And still the handmaids of the Christ
Worked on to shine the brass, and varnished wood,
And the silence seeping from the room
Under the door was thick as any blood.

Forty years on, the boy, the rock of shame
Still hanging from his neck, laid one September night
His head upon the railway line's steel pillow
And slept his way towards the all-obliterating light.

Dead Man in Chipping

There's no one dancing on your grave today, unless
This summer breeze fretting about your plot
Is counterfeit, shapeshifter, and is not
The wind but the troubled restless ghosts
Of those lost boys whose lives you robbed.

They had no voice then in those howling days
In that palace of bad dreams, the college
Where your bloated, princely power held sway;
In those dark corridors carpeted with fear
Your study hung with a great tapestry of tears;
Oak paneled oubliette, reeking of beeswax
Power and shame. I name you now across the years.
It was a pure Catholic Cockayne, sure only Bosch
Could have dreamed up such a topsy turvy world.

You took the glass-clear souls of innocent boys
And dragged them weeping –
Hypocrite priest, demonic spider,
Cassocked, whited sepulcher –
Into the torments of your own dark pit.

And at the monstrous altar's benediction,
In your princely pomp you stood, a pink-faced toad,
And held the monstrance aloft,
Preened and pampered in your silver buckled shoes.
(And let us never forget
The powder for your shining head.)

In a wash of candlelight and frankincense,
The servant of the Carpenter in gold
Embroidered thread and precious stones,
Feigning devotion and pure innocence,
Far louder than the rest, you, Man of God,
Sang out in tuneless tenor from your throne
A cant of love and light, humility
And charity – turning the litany to lies.

Forgiveness not my gift, I traveled here
Only to bear witness to those days;
And as I stand at your graveside,
(Your name in stone still tells no tales),
Head bowed, an old man now,
Alone and hatless in the sun,
I see today that there is no one here with me
Unless the summer whispers in the trees
The soft warm winds that move around this place,
Are revenants, the wandering, unquiet souls
Threading their way down all the days,
The spirits of those once bright, beautiful lost boys.

Sheehan, Deacey, Larkin, Allen and the rest,
We need to name before their stories fade,
Who know no peace, are now one with the wind,
Back from the dead to dance upon your grave.

To the Lighthouse

It happens often in the dark-before-dawn, threshold time,
Those waiting moments when the world shrinks to a breath
Hanging limbo-lost between day's birth and the night's death.
Into the wooded suburbs or some quiet, dull, city street:
There comes a sudden light that streams
Out over roofs and yards, it beats, washes across
The rain-glazed tarmac, the parked cars;
A frantic beacon over seas of sleep.

A mousing cat, perhaps walking a wall, looks up,
Or a worker on his way to early shift
Sees the one light burning over reefs
And shoals of the ordinary, the everyday,
And walks on wondering, perhaps.
Someone is coming, or is going away.

This is a serious light, a light of terror or of tears;
For it brings the wail of sirens, bleating, bleating,
The lamps, cobalt and amber, beating, beating,
Pulsing their way into a world asleep.

The ambulance shudders to a stop, the rear
Doors split open, spilling a brutal blaze
Into the street. A false dawn shines across a sea
Of pain that has no charts, no cipher for
The hapless voyagers on this new passage;
Because each journey is unique there are no maps,
No charts, no angels trumpeting each corner of that world.
A stretcher slithers out, a police car slides up close behind;
The officers climb out to stretch and yawn,
They glance up at the lighthouse, and adjust their caps
And in the East, the slow, light fingerings of the dawn.

Les Parapluies De Manchester

Manchester, midsummer damp, a drizzly day;
On Deansgate – mizzle and a muddling grey;
Glum crowds and car flung puddles drenching passers by
Below the caul of a dour, sour, northern sky.

And the faces swimming past are worn and tired,
Rolling us all on the treadmill of the years
Through the electro-twitter, the crass lies
The half truths, and the alligator tears.

Then to Potato Wharf there comes a sudden burst of carnival,
A gaggle of French children clamorous with delight,
Each carrying one deeply precious, most important thing:
A brightly coloured umbrella shouting hope and joy and light.

Their edges touching on they go crossing by
The fish rib, canal bridge, as in a print by Hokusai,
All sunburst reds, turquoise, leaf-green,
Cobalt, lemon yellow, Burnt Sienna, hot cerise,

Bright colours of the warm South, fairground hues.
A rainbow dragon, on its way to Mardi Gras,
Chatters on bringing to that cold, grey northern street
Smiles to the hearts of those with eyes to see.

The Shipping Forecast

After the gig, leaving behind the beery warmth
Of smoky singing rooms, I rode the blue tar roads;
Nights beyond count I watched the reeling land
Spool past as I drove on, dry eyed and tired always alone,
The rolling ribbon winding out and leading me back home.

The towns and cities left behind
I would cross the country miles and see
The Long Mynd hooded with a cowl of stars,
The wilds of Saddleworth Moor by snowlight
Reaching out in endless waves and folds and bars,
A bleached and noiseless world.
Frost on the Snake, and Shap all furred with fog
So thick you could have knitted it.
One autumn night I stopped on Dunmail Rise
And stood, the land below all lime-lit by a Hunter's Moon,
The only sounds in that still world my breath
And the cooling ticking of the car.

Countless miles and countless times,
Gig done, heading for home,
The radio on, I would comb
Always for company the airwaves;
Searching through the static and the morse,
The ethereal confetti of the universe –
Stations coming and going, babel babble,
Washing like the shorewaves of the sea –
I turned the tuner each night trawling
For the comfort of the human voice,
And settled always on the BBC.

I would follow every word until the very death,
Not hitting the 'Off' switch until
The Shipping Forecast came, that Nunc Dimitis,
That litany of hope and fear, that canticle,
Those words that painted endless oceans
All about the island of my mind:
'Viking, Forties, Tyne, Tiree,
Cromarty, Col, Lundy, Sole,
Shannon, Rockall, Hebrides...'

And as the cats' eyes reeled
Under my wheels I would,
Snug in my own small, warm, tin craft,
See in my mind's eye sailors stood on watch
Out on the widowmaking seas,
Half lit in the wheelhouse.
I saw them smoking, drinking sweet dark tea,
Leaning on the binnacle, eyes locked
On the radar's emerald scrying bowl,
And all ears full-cocked
For the trusted London voice, the oracle:

'Dogger, Fisher, German Bight,
Biscay, Fastnet, Finistere...'
A mantra calling through the night
As deadly serious as any prayer.

The Old Pubs

*Change your hearts or you will lose your inns and you will
deserve to have lost them. But when you have lost your
inns drown your empty selves, for you will have lost the
last of England*

HILAIRE BELLOC, *This and That*, 1912

Rusting shutters blind the windows, stucco
Failing, old brick scabbed and stained, and gutters
Alive with grasses, weeds; small trees are growing
From cold chimneys, the old pubs gone or going.

Singing smoky rooms where out of tune
Joannas gave a Saturday night a little sauce.
Some couples danced while others, dreaming, crooned
Of heartache and romance. Corseted

Grandmothers belted bawdy ballads, old
Geezers, made a few pints braver, rolled
Out something comic and the gang
Knowing every line still laughed and sang

Along. Then, bundling out the door and long goodnights,
The pavements not so steady in the old gaslight;
Still singing quietly, that widow, solo
Gets home feeling somehow less alone.

But algorithms say the ground's worth more for flats
And that, at closing time, is that. Now rats
Skitter through dust, scatter the echoes of lost laughter;
Falling ceilings show the bones of rafters.

In a tower high above it all the suits
With Powerpoint and laptops show a future made
Of glass and steel and bottom lines; the roots
That bind are gone. In town and village

What were once the people's palaces
Wait for the drill and wrecking ball.
Then come the cranes to raise the great-glass phalluses
And you wouldn't know there'd been anything there at all.

Ticking

Only in a certain, sudden light
Can you see the scars, the small, odd marks,
That show the beatings and the sleepless nights
Spent crying, silent, locked up in the dark

Cellar. Only, you can see there is something in the stare
The way he listens, smiles but not at any one thing
You could name. Always there is a pulsing in the air,
Always he holds himself as though about to spring.

They will wonder, when the days are numbered,
When the man grows from the child,
How rough the beast is underneath it all that lumbers,
Slouching out relentless with Bedlam in its eyes.

Easy Enough

Easy enough in the end you'd think:
Get on a train and wave it all goodbye.
Your cup of coffee, half-drunk, lying
Cold, skinned and flat now in the kitchen sink;

The bills unpaid, the letters still unread.
'Looks like he'd had enough.'
They'll say shaking their heads
Over beers and chasers in the pub.

Milk cancelled, all doors locked,
No note, keys posted through the letterbox;
Bus at road end to town, and then the train,
And, as you pull out, light clouds bringing rain.

And you, watching the world slip by –
Gasometers, stone viaducts, the bend
For home – will leave it all behind,
Will step out at the journey's end

To taste salt on the breeze, hear gulls, a seal's bark,
The clabber of waves on shingle and wrack,
And, out in the bay, poised like a question mark,
A single, priestly granite stack.

The Scythe

In the days when they had cloned a sheep
And men had danced across the moon,
When half the dale was still asleep
And the blue bay of the sky was strewn
With the first bright gleanings of the dawn;
As the sun edged up behind the fell
And a curlew called beyond the beck,
You went into the old hay barn
With its green glass windows, cobweb curtained,
The broken cobwebbed bike the bench, the oiled vice,
And you took down your father's scythe
From where you kept it straddling
The wooden pegs spagged in the wall,
And then without a word to any in the house
You wet the stone and lovingly coaxed out
Of the oil-skinned, star bright blade
An edge that could split hairs.

On a field that was near vertical,
At eighty some years old
You mowed all day in the harvest sun,
Mewed the whole damn field alone,
Had footcocks raked and the gleanings in
By the rising of the moon.

And not for profit or for praise or glory
But for the simple, common story
Of a job well done – a craftsman at his craft.
And then, arms aching from your graft,
You rubbed more oil into the blade and shaft
And hung the scythe back up to wait another year.

You stood then, wreathed in pipe smoke in the yard
And heard the owls call your name,
As a satellite blinked amongst the scatter of stars,
Pulsing across the headlands of the dale.

Edge

This is the country town's real edge, just here
Where railway line and river mark
A natural border. And beyond, just fields,
A flood plain and a hill a half mile off,
Topped with a crust of Yorkshire stone,
A hamlet with a church, a closed Post office,
A reading room and a dead pub.

And in between the hamlet and the town? This nothing,
This wilderness of riches: flowers and stoats
And hares and hedgehogs, badgers,
Oystercatchers, curlews and the stiff schoolmaster
Hunch of the grey heron waiting for the class
Of fry and salmon parr to come his way.
Dippers dive, wagtails bob, kingfishers flit
Trailing their lapis thread across the air.

And in this nothing there is all of England:
The fields pieced by five hundred years of graft,
The banks cut straight by monks so they could smear
The flats with golden barley; then the sheep
And cattle came. It is rough flood land, rich
Though still in silt and loam and sedge.
Old Yorkshire; men bled here, battles won and lost
Became the matter of a fireside tale. The edge.

And now the hoardings tell
Us there will be 'Executive Homes.
Exclusive.' And the planners
And the draughtsmen and the bankers,
And the builders all shake hands
As the town crawls slowly out across the land.

And the young leave, and the old stay,
And the river swells a little more each year.
And there are men who see such land and say,
'It's only some old fields. There's plenty here.'
But money is Time's whore and field by field
The land is lost, the animals die or go away,
The birds are silent. Soon the only noise will be
The yarl of mowers and the wailing strimmers
Sending out their empty, monied songs
Across the summer lawns, the slowly rising river.

Miley's Story

'Just a few feet higher they'd have made it,'
Miley said, setting his cap back on his head,
His pint down hard upon the foam-ringed wood.
 'We heard it right here in this pub that night.
We knew it were no good, it were too low. Shite
Weather, mizzle, fog and rain and cloud.
And then there was the bang. My God! So bloody loud!
You know, we thought it were a bomb!
But it was the plane hittin' the crags.'
He took a sip then wiped his mouth
'They were makin' for somewhere down south.'

But something happened that foul night
That threw them all awry
And sent them here into the Dales, a sacrifice,
Low on fuel and flying blind
Those final few miles through a sea of milk.
What panic they'd have known
Those Canadian bomber boys. Then came
The caterwauling engines and the hit.
Then another world of silence and the sky
Above the Meggerstones lit by the spilt fuel fire.

The Home Guard mustered and, with Miley's horse,
Set off to bring them down; a small khaki cortege
Of farmers' lads and shepherds dragged the dead
Boys down the fell, their bier an old hay sledge.
'Not a mark upon em.' Miley said, 'Not a scratch;
It were just as though they all were fast asleep.'

Hanging on the wall in The Sun today,
(A dwindling band still know its tale)
Is the great horse collar taken from the neck
Of Miley's big old horse, used to haul them off
The fell that killing night through drizzle and through fog.
Now ramblers on Great Combe, from time to time,
Find rivets, shards of scabrous aluminium, perspex,
And wonder at these relics of the wreck,
These scattered, votive offerings to the gods
Of fell and dale and war and tarn and bog.

Our Willie

Born covered with the caul of shame
They kept you secret, hidden
15 years, a cuckoo chicken
In a coop. Who even knew your name?
That you existed? Breathed? Walked? Spoke?
Unschooled, told to hide,
That your mother was your sister,
Thinking the world outside
A kaleidoscope of changing lights and fears.
You wandered through the spinning years;
Your borders: fell end and the stars,
Holes in the lampblack roof that held your world.

Shut away when strangers came:
The parson or the ministry men,
Lost walkers rambling off the moor.
Over the years the village grew
To know your story but their lips
Stayed closed, your epic local
A nod, a wink and nothing said to strangers.

When you emerged full grown,
(Blinking we must assume)
With no maps for this new made world,
You nonetheless knew all the names and ways
Of every living creature
In the scattered acres
Of your high part of the dale, but little else.

Uncertain in a world bounded by stone and bog
You worked the land, serf-like, until it fell away
In ledger lines and was sold off above your head.
Then you became in time a local character,
An old man in your corner in the pub.
You rarely spoke – except to note
The weather or something you'd seen
An otter sliding eel like from the bank into a beck,
Or Falcons, feathered bombs up on the combe's high ledge.

A clay pipe sucked, a few gills drunk,
And that was just about the measure of it all.
A life half-lived, a secret sharer,
Feral almost, able barely to talk,
Able just about to make his mark
Within a few cramped acres of the dale, his holy ground;
The dale's secret a lost boy, never lost and never found.

Jackie Two Sticks

Saw you this moisty morning:
Molecatcher Jackie, two sticks and a dog.
Fog rolling in a slow flood down the dale;
And you, Jack In The Mist, pooled pale
Between the trees lapping
The swollen river's banks,
You came through the milky light tapping
Your way a stick in each bent bird-claw hand

Jackie One Stick when I saw you last,
Jackie No Stick when I saw you first,
The day I came to live here, thirty-some years past.
Time's sickle garners everything,
And now, just like the moles you trapped,
You tap your slow, myopic way towards the last
Haytime, last calling in, the churchyard bend
You and your moles, Jackie, together at the end.

Brothers in the Frost

The wall is furred and skinned with frost,
A young bull calf goes skittering on the cobbles,
Stumbles, steadies then, on shit-caked hooves,
Hobbles on the ice glazed track;
Shakes its poll, eyes dazed, mad,
Breath from its muzzle smoking.
Crust of cat ice in the raw wheel ruts,
Sun a pale bleb on the crag's black edge,
Sedge frozen at the lake's still lip.

Two brothers side by side, coat-less
Lead on the prancing bull.
Bald though young, their faces grey with dirt,
Leery, gap-toothed, unshaven grins;
Their clothes tom-cat rank
With months of wearing.

This could be a Breugel come to life
In browns and ochres with a touch
Of rose about the noses and the ivory of frost.
They stump unseeing past a string of long dead moles
Strung, shriveled, hanging like
A row of frozen socks hung from
Barbed wire that tops the drystone wall.

They walk bow-legged into a future
Not of rockets, moonwalks, silicon chips,
But marts and sales and mud and shit.
Nothing touches them, they are the rocks
The roots, the weather; digger bucket teeth,
The price of till, and dip, the cost of a new bull

Is all their craft and care.
Red diesel is their world, they wear a shell
Of country daft and stand apart at every sale,
Mocked by the knowing nudges, winks – and yet
They've brass enough to buy up half the dale.

A Dalesman's Litany

He knows each inch and every half-inch of the land,
Each outcrop, every field, each stand
Of trees. This is it: his kingdom, bailiwick.
He walks these windy acres with his stick

And dog. Were he stone-blind he yet would know each wall,
Each field, by its own voice, its whisper and its call:
Wind songs in every tree, the cry of each small syke,
The chant of every spring and freshet, pool and dyke.

He is the last can read and parse this windy dale
(The fields and barns not named on any chart)
Yet draws back diving into silence like a snail
Under the salt of strangers questions. He has the land by heart.

Schooled by the fells about he hoards the rubric in his blood:
His lexicon, word book – the fields, barns, crags.
His gazetteer's not one you'd find in any guide or map –
Jaggers Way, Dub Foss and Hard Bought Wood,

Lord's Rake and Peacock's Barn, Burnt Syke.
From the twisted thorn in the limestone gryke
To the rowans in the high outrake – each mountain mile
His litany, each gate and gap, each cripple hole and stile.

And when he goes the book will be no more,
The story of the land gone like a sputtering candle flame,
Snuffed out, with all its legends, tales and names,
Lost in time's wind and the future's careless open door.

Collier – the Enemy Within

He lies side on, near naked in a two-foot seam,
Man-foetus, hacking out the light of ancient suns.
A mile above him laughing children dam the stream,
The hedges hang their may, the wild hare runs.

Coiled in the Davy Lamp dark he hews the coal, cuts
Out the bright black jewels that fire the dreadnought's screw,
That smelt the bullets' lead, and forge the iron boots
That police the Empire's bounds. Hutched

In the halo of the lamp's gold, lambent light,
Curled, bent, he chops the boles of forests from a time
When giant lizards walked the Earth.
And high above him in the summer-day's bright warmth

The kings of the New Jerusalem walk the links,
Adjust their grips, address the ball, while in his black
Tomb deep below, naked but for rags, the enemy within
Hacks on, the weight of kings and empires on his back.

The Island of Cockaigne

The Bluebird, Sialia sialis, is not found in Europe

Getting here was easy, I didn't have to move
A foot; the country shifted round me overnight.
One shove and we were in another place
Where up is down, and grey is white,
And you can have and eat your endless cake.

Daughters and sons of Albion, old Billy Blake
Will wonder where it all went queer,
This land of warm spinsters and beer,
The cycling churches, morning mist and spam,
Spitfires and bungalows, Jerusalem and jam.
But worry not The Wicked Witch come from the East
One stroke has felled, the bitch is now deceased.

In this Island of Cockayne the pigs
Run round with knives, cutting from off their own
Arses shives of most delicious ham,
Flicking them them, dead-eye, into the frying pan.
The chickens now lay soft boiled eggs, trees pick
Their own fruit, and the spuds all resurrect
Themselves as down the sky there comes a hail
Of toasted Cheddar cheese. The lager fountains play
All day, the cigarette trees never fail,
The pitbulls all have rubber teeth, the sun
On this empire always forgets to set,
And nobody grows old or mad or ails.

Ah what a land we have now that we have it back!
Took forty years of lies to cut the cable.
(What's on the table? Feck-all Mabel.)
The headless chickens are egg bound,
The sages read the entrails and have found
The cupboard bare, that everything is gone,
The pilots left the ship they sank
(After clearing out the bank)
Singing the Eton Boating Song.

But the clouds rain chocolate money now,
And the rivers of beer flow free,
Full English served all round the clock
And plenty honey still for tea.
I think I hear the mermaids singing
To the bluebirds, each to each,
'Bon voyage! Soyez calme!' they sing
On the strand at Dover Beach.

Balmoral, Scotland, 1912

Up to her elbows in gizzards and crops,
Livers, sweetbreads giblets and hearts, a kitchen maid
Pokes back a sweaty straying lock;
The cooks hack heads, chop limbs. A blade,

Pure Sheffield steel, unseams a hare – slits,
Goes in, slides up, twists. Pigs' heads,
Feathers, fins, goose down, sweetbreads –
The flags are slick with blood and sweat and shit.

Fires roar, stoves bark, crack and belch;
Clouds of flesh-pink steam writhe
And roil around the great kitchen, and men
Heap fuel on fuel, feeding the bloody, hungry fires.

All day on the estate the guns and rods are out,
Killing pheasants, ducks, salmon and sea trout.
The trains and carriages are bringing the great men
Sazonov and Grey, His Majesty, Haldane –

The men of silence who talk much behind closed doors,
Who finger maps and, pacing polished floors,
Talk of the North Sea, tonnage – riddling out the sands –
And speak of how the next great slaughter must be planned.

Five years of butchering, and where it led:
The old world's gross dismantling more or less –
Was decided over dinner here by these wise heads,
Between the sea trout entrée and the Eton Mess.

And a Nightingale Sang

The BBC still have it in their vaults:
Birdsong recorded in a Surrey wood.
Summer '42, a long day drawing to its close,
And clear as moonlight, singing at the spinney's heart:
A nightingale, its bubbling song, liquid
Crystal, the eternal music of the stars.

That long-dead bird, that relict wood,
That summer's night, you can hear them still,
Fixed on magnetic tape, frozen in time,
The kiss of breeze and leaves, that lilting bird
They go out singing yet across Time's hill.

Then, as you listen, slow, behind
The birdsong grows the groan,
A murmur first and then a moan:
The caoin of heavy bombers heading for the coast
Their bellies fat, fecund with Death.
The two songs weave, both warp and weft,
In that Surrey summer's night into a perfect kōan.

Somehow the engineer that night,
His tape spools rolling, and his mic
Hooded in its parabolic cowl,
Searching for the eternal in the trees,
Found the most beautiful of all birdsongs,
And then, by happenstance, the howl,
The savage tribal chant of War's mad wrongs.

Listen to the two strains still:
The music fluting from the nightingale
Singing out the world's strange mystery;
And then the other, counterpoint, chill:
The immutable, absurd and murderous wail
Of the making of Mankind's mad history.

Night Shunting

We children lay there huddled in the dark
Beneath old army greatcoats in the still, cold room,
Outside the winter trees were dancing skeletons, stark
Against the full face of the hunting moon.

The rattle of trucks came from the marshalling yards
Across from our street, a fussy iron rosary
That cackled, shuttled, clanked and barged
To a standstill in the sidings. Presently

More trucks were shunted, rolling down
The line until the train became an iron snake
That stretched beyond the streets, out of the town.
The engineer released the brake,

The hissing dragon growled and huffed,
We saw the sparks escape, swirl free above it all,
As the firebox brushed a wash of burning blood
Across the canvas of our little bedroom wall.

We heard the downstairs voices through the wooden boards
Of our bare bedroom floor. He roared,
'I tell you it is cattle – fool!' pointing to the dark,
Outside 'Just cattle! Cattle!' Beating exclamation marks

With his fists upon the table. We listened as the train
Rolled off into the future, leaving us behind. The full moon bled
Through Jack Frost flowers on the window pane –
'But, cattle don't speak Yiddish' was all our mother said.

King of The Bulldozers, Belsen 1945

By some strange miracle it didn't rip his soul
From out his body, send it howling down
Across the barbed wire and the huts,
The soup kitchens, the staring ghouls.
You'd think that young swaddie,
Who worked the levers with such skill,
Sending a jumbled hill of flesh
And bones and grinning papered skulls
Into the pit to meet the lime of History,
Would have been led away stark mad.

But no, that soldier and bulldozer,
The exhaust yammering, sucked
His Woodbine lowered his blade again,
And pushed another mound of Jews
And Gypsies, Communists and Gays
Into the pit, because that was
The most humane and loving,
Caring thing he could have done:
That tender turning down of earth
Over the sticks and meat and rags
That had once laughed and loved
And sung and breathed and been.

Perhaps we ought to get down on our knees
And plead with any God you please
That in these lunatic days
That tender Woodbine smoker,
King of the Bulldozers,
Never has to comfort us
Or those we love that way.

Oppenheimer's Cézanne

Oh it's true he tried to poison his professor,
And it's true he taught the physicists to sin (not that
They needed that much teaching – what with mustard gas,
Anthrax, napalm and phosphorous.) And it's a fact
That he declared, from the Bhagavadgita these eight words
As the monstrous mushroom flowered from the desert floor,
'Now I am become Death, destroyer of worlds.'

And yet he was, it seems, all times, a shy and quiet man
Who never came to grips quite with the world;
The money and the pandering saw to that.
So when he crashed the car, his girlfriend by his side,
(She was bruised and shocked – but no-one died)
It didn't take too much to fix. His folks,
Afraid his future might be canned,
To buy her silence only coughed up one quite small Cézanne,
And happily, of course, it didn't break the bank.

Compared to Einstein he was second rank,
But he found that he could rule, could oversee,
And under his command they mined the mother lode.
In moonshine country, Oak Ridge, Tennessee
They unpicked Pandora's code, first found the magic key,
Unlocked the box and painted Pandemonium
Across the soft, blue, early morning Japanese sky.

This time it surely would have cleared them out –
In my mind's ear I hear his parents shout,
'Hiroshima! Nagasaki! Sweet Jehosaphat
Julius! how many fucking Cezannes is that?'

Snowdrops

Three splintered stumps, all that's left of a relict wood
Old before Napoleon's men marched here,
And as their base, an island in this sea of frozen mud,
A raft of grass, withered by winter, drear

And seeming without life. Yet amongst the tufts of dead
And glassy blades: he sees the nodding ivory bells
Of snowdrops, a peal, a dozen heads,
Hardly more. They speak to him of Spring, tell

Him there's a better, different world
Beyond this lunacy, where Sal, his girl
Back home still waits for him. So Harry plucks
A handful, sticks them in his cap for luck.

Later that day lugging a box of ammo
To the front, he stops for breath. And so
Jürgen the sniper sees the sudden flash
Of white just like the third light from the match,
A panicked rabbit's tail. And workmanlike, a sandbag for a
    prop,
He nails the rabbit, scatters the snowdrops.

The Sudden Conversion of C S Lewis in a Sidecar on the Road to Whipsnade Zoo

I rode, well coddled underneath an old plaid rug,
Snug in the shuddering sidecar of
The motorbike my brother drove,
(A Royal Enfield two-five-oh, I think it was.)
We trundled nicely through the streets that day,
Off for a lark. I, sensing nothing strange
Or odd, perched there smug, with flying sparks
Like tiny devils leaping from my pipe
At every bump and lurch. My hat jammed on my head
Scarf round my neck, gloves on, cold nose.
We passed a church, a synagogue, a chapel. Ripe?
I must have been for something; Newton's Apple? I suppose.

We overtook a charabanc, four cyclists, three
Nuns and then, about halfway to Whipsnade
(As though, while swimming in a cold dark sea
I'd happened on a warm safe bay)
There came the day-plain certainty
There was one God, who ruled over eternity,
Who always was and is and will forever be;
His only truly begotten Son, the man-god Jesus
Had sacrificed himself upon the cross to save us.

I noticed that my pipe was out, the ash all blown,
And so we clattered on into a stranger zoo made all
Of talking badgers, ice queens, portal wardrobes,
Centaurs, lamp posts, lions, silent planets and The Fall.

Angels and Air

Once I built a tower leading to the sun
Brick and rivet and lime
Once I built a tower, now it's done
Brother, can you spare a dime?

E.Y. 'YIP' HARBURG

They are there still, on that hot day in New York:
Angels on a lunch-break from their work;
Hawk high, perched way above the earth,
Suspended both in time and space;
Sitting it seems on air, wings folded back,
Their working-stiff smiles,
Their careless roosting grace,
Fixed in the frozen moment of the photograph.

Fearless, and yet fallen, they dance on
Eleven angel-men at lunch what seems
A teem of miles above the world.
The city far below rubbed smooth
By the summer's pall, where all
The Polaks, Spics and Paddies,
Italian barbers, Ashkenazi Rabbis,
Kraut hash slingers, blind street singers,
Hookers, ramblers, Chinese gamblers,
High class whores, hustlers and bores,
Are rooting for their dollars in the roaring streets.

Heat raddles the fallen; the Irish cops,
Frazzled, mop their Cork and Kerry brows,
Slam night-sticks into slán-segged Connemara hands;
And black, zoot-suited dudes, the Jazz
Kings of the Harlem night come forth. They are
The coked up brass men, wide eyed bass men,
Cold-turkey crooners of the Cotton Club;
Their hours come again, all are re-born,
And surface blinking, slouching like rude beasts
Into the megapolis of the morning light.

And the city moils in its own great greenback mill,
Not knowing there are angels up on high,
Cherubim with riveter's mitts, still
Perched upon the girder: seraphim with spanners,
Munching on their bagels, their pastrami on rye.
A quick draw on their Lucky Strikes
And then they don their wings again,
And set to work dragging New York
Up from the roots, new Babel,
Trumpeting its hallowed destiny,
Rivet by rivet, inching ever up and on
Towards the unattainable, blue, dreamer's sky.

The Three Ivans

They sit on car seats ripped from the staff car,
Kings of the dust and rubble,
A fine mahogany door on bricks their table,
Ivan and his friend, Ivan, their helmets off,
Eating the good sausage and bread they've taken from
The Gruppenführer they've just killed, drinking from tin cups
The delicate Gewürztraminer found in his attaché case.

The body of their benefactor lies, headless, still warm,
Keeping the flies from this their banquet in the ruins.
His chauffeur, a Hitlerjugend, just seventeen years,
Lies close by in the smoking dust, his head still on
Though most of what had been his face is gone;
His mother might just know him by his ears.

There is war and fighting still in distant streets,
The crack of sniping, grenades, machine guns bleat;
But not here, no not here, this is a still calm pool,
Peaceful, free of flying lead. Ivan's bayonet
Cuts two more shives of bread
From off the loaf as oily, sooty flecks

That once had been the Führer settle on the crust,
Their brows, their shoulders, speck their wine.
The other Ivan, his mouth full of pork,
Führer and bread says, 'It looks like rain,
I tell you what Ivan old chum,
I'll be glad when all this shite is done
And I'm back on the farm again.'

A sudden tank comes snarling, sees them sitting there,
Among the great stone eagles, tumbled porticos, smashed walls.
The driver, another Ivan, gives thumbs up then gives a wave
As the party in the ruins raise their cups and toast the day.
And the Führer and his mädchen fleck the air
Falling in flakes of black snow on the smouldering square.

The Last 'K' in Kirkuk

Kids at 'The Flicks' we loved the cowboy films,
Bouncing on the dusty seats as they spun the reel
And shafts of light and dark made stories on the silver screen.
There were big fights with Indians and Outlaws and
The Texas Rangers. In our small world the Cavalry
Always arrived in time, the goodies wore white hats,
The baddies black – and that was that.
Often the films would open with a map
Of Mexico or Texas, the debatable lands,
Indian territory; lines drawn with a pen, freehand.
Then a flame would crawl relentlessly across the chart
And we knew that this was where the real epic would start.

Just so two men with a ruler and a pen
In secret talks (as Europe sent its sons
To slaughter, a generation drowned in lies and paper)
Unpicked an Empire. Carrion crows in suits,
Monsieur Picot and Sir Mark Sykes with great
Urbanity cut up the crumbling Ottoman cake.

And now the scholars scour, decode the secret screeds;
Historians pore, destroy their sight
Unravelling the web: the treaties, declarations,
The Arabs, Zionists, the League of Nations.
And still it comes down to just this: two men, a map.

And in that room in Downing Street
A handsome man, (silky moustache,
Bright eyes, an element of dash,
How ironic that his name was Mark,)
With a ruler and a chinagraph
Drew lines of fires to come across the chart.

Bred in the bone, born to the breed,
Sykes smiling in the waning light, said, 'Look,
I should like to draw a straight line from the "e"
In Acre to the last "k" in Kirkuk.'

Prayers of the Great Despoilers

1   The Hymn of Dynsdale

Lord thou knowest how my charge doth tax me,
How day on day in the ploughpath of thy work, waxing
Wroth in justified contempt I labour, filled with zeal
And ardour. Uncomplaining, from thy cause I never shirk.
Thy storm bringer am I, my cataracts and hurricanoes blast
The filth from out thy holy halls. I ride each dawn
My list clutched in my fist; my true
Disciples: hammer, bar and hook. Acres of glass
Will fall like brittle flocks of wounded birds
To the plain song of my blows, the vain idolatrous
Gewgaws like rainbow devils will come singing to the floor
As thou did cast the fallen angels down.
(Thou knowest that we get tuppence a bucket
For it from Wilkins the glazier in the town)
Glass I shatter, stone I sunder,
The thunder of my cohorts' hammers sends
The idols crashing, faces smashed, noses trashed,
Knights on their tombs, vain even in death,
We level, unmaking them in a breath.

Oh but how my heart lusts for thee Lord
As my hammer sings its psalm.
And Lord how zealous I was and dutiful too;
So little time and yet so much to do.
How could we turn in months
The apostasy of the ages?
Yet I laboured for Thee hacking off
The faces of the saints – false idols, angels,
All that riotous flesh those colours.

For yea my God is bleak, the God of Plague and Storm.
With tempest and sores and vengeance let Him rule.
Let Him bring an end to rainbows, bring in grey on grey
And let those painted saints and stinking Virgins
With their sky blue cloaks go find another haven.

Let us leave them all in bright scatterings about the abbey
    floors
Nowt but clear glass showing grey skies
Nowt but black
Nowt but white.

My job is simple, Lord. I am Thy hammer.
I am Armageddon come to tear, to trump the works
Of days and hands. We scour and scrape
And yet the work of many days and many hands
It is to clear the glass alone.
But still I labour on.
And so I, thy despoiler goes each dawn,
Embracing the dull grey
Of this poor flesh hoping only to pass
Beyond in time into thy heavenly garden
Where I hope thou wilt
Thy servant Bless
And all his vile sins Pardon.
Amen.

2 The Song of Dalton

We read how Cyril of Alexandria
Father of the early church
Jealous in the Love of God
Zealous in thy worship and thy creed
Sent five hundred Nitrian monks
Hooded and armed into the city;
How they took, without pity,
Glorious in their love
For Thee who reigns above,
The woman Hypatia, daughter of Theon,
Finest woman mathematician,
Finest teacher – yet a woman
Sack of dung, stinking of fish,
And far worse, a pagan –
How they took her from her chariot
In the streets of that city of scholars.

And we read how they took shards
Of broken crockery and in Thy holy name,
Prayers coming with their every breath,
They did carefully and joyously, the same
Priests, exulting in Thy works, scrape her to death.

So Lord let me scrape clean thy holy house,
Scour it of false idols, so that the rude
And superstitious might,
In plain and holy white,
Give praise to Thee
And to Thy Guiding Light.
Amen.

The Wrong Turning – Schiller's Deli

Four young men (boys almost) came that day
To bring the whole of Europe to its knees.
Mehmedbašić couldn't draw his gun they say,
Čubrilović went home, not happy, not at all at ease –
Sorry for the Archduke's wife,
Her soft brown curls, her pretty dress.
10.10am, Čabrinović, lobbed his bomb and messed
His throw, instead blew up the car behind,
He bit a glass capsule of cyanide
That merely made him sick, and so he threw
Himself into the Miljacka river which was dry;
They dragged him out, muddy, bruised but still alive.

So enraged was the Archduke Ferdinand
That, after meeting the Lord Mayor,
Shaking several dignitaries hands
And offering up a thankful prayer,
He ordered the chauffeur to drive straightway
To the hospital where all the wounded lay.

But the driver, Lojka, confused, took a wrong
Turn, realised his fault, reversed and stalled
The car and found himself mired in a lake of blood,
Cadavers, grinning skulls and mud,
Stuck in a sea of body parts beneath a pall,
The gathering dark skies of the years to come.

11.30am outside Shiller's Deli across the street
The fourth boy Princip saw the frozen motorcade,
Took out his Belgian pistol, and in two heartbeats
Laid his imprimatur on the face of all our days.

One student, two shots placed so neatly,
Dried signatures on parchment treaties –
 All it took to set the old world burning:
A befuddled chauffeur, and the wrong turning.

History Lesson

I read in history books about The Treaty Of This,
The Accord of The Other, the Annexations,
Conferences, alliances, the mobilisations;
But in my mind's eye all I see this:

Old men and women their lungs full of ice,
Licking the frost from all that's left not burned,
The grass that grows in ruts in the blackened earth.
I see children trying to melt a seed head in a frozen pond.

I do not see the flags or hear the bands,
Or see, in high rooms, great men signing, pens in hand,
Nor do I see the men with ribbons on their chests;
I see a women trying to feed a child with empty breasts.

No I don't see the victories, applaud your glory,
Or hear your cheers; my kind of story
Hears the screams of rape, sees the pogrom's tears,
The villages burned, that's what comes screaming down the
    years.

So sound your trumpets, bang your drums;
Over all your mad vainglorious shouts,
The cries of history must always come
To drown your howls of victory out.

Belfast Flight – 1979

Once the wheels tucked in the stranger smiled, hands
On a small case nestled on his lap – red morocco leather,
Size of a good book. We talked about the weather,
Then why we both were heading out to Ireland.

He was a surgeon – neonates – he specialised
In newborn babies' hearts; those tiny intense scraps
Of barely breathing us, mankind, were all his care.
He opened up the case 'I have invented these – so rare.

There are no others like them anywhere.'
Lying slotted in silk, minute, precise, Love's jewels:
The tiniest of scissors, scalpels, forceps, clamps,
Finest Sheffield steel, a Lilliputian craftsman's tools.

'I carry them with me always. A tiny hole is all I need
To mend the broken hearts.' Alone in all the world
This man: in all the world this one small case
Of love, these straw-thin, silver wands of healing.

'I make them in my shed.' he told me with a smile.
The plane canted to turn, wings dipped; across the miles
Of streets we saw the towers, the armoured cars,
Bombed streets, barbed wire, the city's beating heart.

Hindu Kush Prince – Chitral 1992

I sat once in a garden with a prince, a quiet old man,
Around us were the high peaks of the Hindu Kush
A broken moonscape, land of rock and dust.
Yet ice-melt water from high glaciers ran

In mile on mile of stone-lined leats to make a sweet
Still paradise here, this bower with walnut trees,
And apricots and grass. We sat for hours, a warm breeze
Danced the branches, and then the sandaled feet

Of a shuffling *chai wallah* meant that tea was here,
Not doodh chai – Twinings tea. This prince, last of his kind
    to rule,
Had travelled four days on a horse each year
To the railhead, then the train to England and his school.

He showed me photos – cricket flannels, blazer,
A rowing cap. His library here (the damp in winter
Worried him) was leather bound: Ovid, Shakespeare,
Milton, Pope, but now, 'My eyes are dim and hazy,

I do not read as I once used.' His palace
Was a fort of mud and rock and logs, and yet
His towels came from Selfridges, a friend, 'alas
Now dead' sent them each year. 'And how is London now?'

He asked, this prince of rubble, king of dust.
'Owned by the Russians, most of it.' I said
'Ah yes,' he shook his head. 'The Taliban
Kicked their backsides and they went home

And turned their empire upside down. The CIA
And MI6 they made the mujahideen and it,
Just like the scorpion, will turn and sting them
When they least expect. Try these,' he pointed

'They are scones, not like your English ones
We cannot get the flour. But they remind me of
Old Oxford and the Cotswold hills, cream teas –
I had a bicycle.' He smiled, the sun moved round,

Long shadows fell across the lawn,
A cool wind shook the marigolds in their beds,
Somewhere the rumble of a large rockfall,
And the slow groan of the glacier at the valley's head.

Lines Written in a Country Churchyard

The headstones trumpet all their certainties,
So doubtless were they that on Judgement Day
They would be re-assembled, living once again,
Liver, lights and bones for all eternity.
Full fleshed but stumbling, slightly dazed,
They'd clamber out of their several graveyard slots,
Looking for the ladder that would raise
Them up unto the right hand of their God.

My own faith gone I know they rot, are dust
No Maker's trump will wake; no Heaven waits, no Hell.
Across the dying day the evening bell
Tolls out across God's Little Acre,
And the autumn sun tells out the names
Of the good mulch that lies below. The worms
Are dancing, only words remain and they,
The *Jacobs, Jessicas, Ruths*
And *Benjamins* in time will wear away.
Already they are difficult to read;
Lichen picks, frost flakes the stone,
The mason's work undone
By the soft and silent chisel of the years.

Yew trees and church, a quintessential English scene
That meant so much to those who knew its code;
And now it's hard to see just what it means.
In churches across this land the story hardly holds:
The porch with wire nets to stop the martin's nest;
Inside, box pews and regimental flags,
Stale flowers on a dusty windowsill,
Mouse droppings, the still, echoing damp,
Tapestry kneelers, noseless faces
Stare down from corbels at the brass lectern
And the old churchwarden's mace.
There is, in every hallowed place,
The marble wall plaque with the list of boys
Who marched away mates, smiling and were lost.

Someone is burning leaves, smoke pricks my eyes,
Somewhere beyond the trees a tractor turns,
Making its way homewards as the dusk comes on.
I sit as night rolls in, certain only that
There is the one certainty: that Time brings
All of us in time to something much like this:
The silent marble naming stones
Ranked in their faithful rows,
Over the rotting bones,
Under the high, old, English oaks
And the calls of homecoming rooks.

May Funeral

'He would have liked it here' they say
Settling their handbags on their laps
Dabbing their eyes, checking their hats;
'The flowers are beautiful but it's cold for May.
Is that the cousin that went to the bad?
Always a rum 'un was that lad.'

The silencing bulk of coffin on the bier
Is faux brass handles, shining oak veneer.
Candles dance in the chill May breeze
As a plaster god hangs from the cross
Looks down on grief implacably,
And someone sat beneath it coughs.

A child sniffles as the vicar mouths
Words worn down like old stones.
They aren't churchgoers, 'But you have
To mark the passing, pay the ferryman
With something do you not?'
They take the body on a trolley to the plot.

The empty sky stretches across
Acres of stone angels, cherubs, marble urns.
They trundle in procession following no one,
Throw crumbs of earth and clay and weep.
The council men move in the JCB
To fill the hole. Coughs and quiet handshakes
As they shuffle down the paths feeling the gathering cold
To see a scratch upon the summer sky
An airliner, oblivious to all their griefs bound for the pole.

Murder Mile Créperie

Hello I'm Clovis, come to show you round
This basement flat, half underground.
You get the sun at least four weeks a year,
What's that I heard you say my dear?

Well half a mill's the guide price; bids
Already in have more than covered it.
You'll need yours in by Tuesday at the latest.
The plaster? A little damp, agreed, it's not the greatest.

Ah now I see you nod, you smile, and yes
This Hackney street *was* once called 'murder mile'
But where once you had stabbings, fights and rapes
We now have sushi, artisan bread and crêpes.

We'll have to hurry now if you don't mind,
There's twelve more couples coming close behind.

Lunar Caustic

Moon paintings, junk shop photographs,
The jetsam of the years,
Car boot sale albums, sepia prints
They vault the everyday, the now,
To resurrect the stories of the past:
The legends, myths the fables of us all.
Something as simple as the picture of a jaunt
Perhaps – a smiling group sat in a charabanc,
About to set off for a day out at the sea;
Work hands shade eyes against the sun, one head
A blur, she turned just as the shutter blinked.
A couple on a motorbike about to leave on honeymoon
Look in the lens as though they're searching for
The path through to the years to come.
A first communion, a shy boy, velvet pants,
Black patent leather shoes, silk shirt, gloved hands
Hold rosary beads, stares as though hiding a hurt.
A gypsy wedding the men stiff in suits,
The bride – white flowers in her hair;
Three fiddlers, moustached and solemn
Hold their violins like guns.
That working girl, all stiff and vulnerable,
Cloche hat over auburn curls
Smiles shyly in her Sunday best.
That private with his gun and khaki battledress
Standing at arms before a painted world;
Soon he'll exchange that for a land
Of ice and madness, lice and mud
From which we know somehow he won't return.

Something so very special at those moments when
The shutter opened like a flower, the lens
Bent light, the moon's soft silver salts fused
Accepting the image like a kiss or bruise.

And now, the last links to their legends lost,
The everyday becomes iconic,
Like Easter Island faces they stare out
From albums in back street junk shops,
Snapshots, ranked random in their jumbled piles.
Cave paintings, petroglyphs and Inca lines;
Each image a serious, undeniable mystery.
The chronicle we sense rather than know; they bring
The epics of the universal to the everyday.
We hang on them the chains of History, of fable,
These paintings from the blind side of the moon.

Lunar Caustic – Silver Nitrate, once the basis of all photography.
Ancient alchemists associated silver with the moon. In the age
of digital photography, we have forgotten film, prints,
darkrooms enlargers, but once much of the silver in the world
went into making images of the most extraordinary everyday.

Hamlet in Ribblesdale

Something rotten in the state all right.
You don't need a graveyard-mouldy skull
To tell you that, to tell you wrong from right.
There is a very old English verb, 'to gull'.

It means 'to swindle, dupe or con.'
It is the smirk of tricksters, money making
Hucksters, 'Find-the-lady' men, who flog
The pig and poke and rent you back the bacon.

They spout morality and probity while still
They're armpit deep in the money cow's arse,
Slipping out their own fat golden calf. Well
Honestly you'd have to laugh at the farce,

But for the tragi-comic fact
That well before the final act
(The poison scene, Ophelia in the rushes)
They have skedaddled, left behind just
Cigar smoke and mirrors, hushed
The clamour of the voices, gone offshore.
The great cash cow, the state they milked
And hated is no more, kaput, defunct,
The whole shebang has been flogged off
And settled down offshore.
(Rosencrantz and Guilderstien, well bilked,
Back from the food bank sleep now in a cardboard bed
(A neon plough and stars blinks overhead.)

There's nothing left today but rude mechanicals
In donkey's heads who have been well and truly led
By the bread and circus nose, and bled
Dry by the market's cogs tyrannical.
They find themselves not in some bosky wood
With Titania and Peaseblossom and Puck,
But standing on the stone-cold flags of Elsinore
Naked, gulled and rooked and out of luck,
And wearing the serf's motley one time more.

Omertà

The blood it never dried on the baton, boot or lathi
Whether what lay below was Irish bog, the veldt,
Or the slag of a northern mine. 'Our duty
Must be done,' they said, and in they went.

And after took the records by the ton and burned
And buried them, the words pecked out, redacted
By the clerks, and ministers, a whole sub-section of the tribe,
In dusty rooms, fans fly-specked whirring overhead,

Geckos watching, clinging to the walls,
As scissors and blue pencils did their work.
Paper Himalayas, shipped out to the fires,
Erased the past in Kenya, Orgreave, Amritsar.

The omertà rich and heady still hangs around the throne,
It stalks the corridors tacit, it's in their very bones;
And the citizens of nowhere see the three
Wise monkeys steer us where they will.

The schools, the colleges, the ministries,
It matters less which path you took than that
You come to eat the bread, and sup the wine
In the communion of the more than willing dumb.

So comes the flags, the Cenotaph, the mythos
Of the cricket field, the lie the Empire told us to the end:
'We were good people.' All I hear
Is the beat of lorries carrying the truth,

The villages burned, the balls and tongues cut off,
The rapes, the sodomies, the swaddies manning red hot guns,
The hangings, floggings, the blood pooling in the dust,
The bog, the streets, the children burned alive.

I hear the engines grumbling to the fires, the gentle click
Of ice cubes in the G and T on the verandah;
As the truth goes up in smoke warm breezes stir the jacaranda
In a world whose underpinning was the briefing and report

The carbon copies, the sealed bag. Facts, dates and names;
Shelf on shelf the ribboned files went marching to the flames,
And in the valley of the willful blind a new-born Calvinism
    stalks
The land, and there are always things of which we must not
    talk.

Italian *Omertà* – (among the Mafia) a code of silence about
criminal activity and a refusal to give evidence to the police.

Pipe Tunes

And they would, after battle, craft a tune, worry the notes,
Badger them until they bloomed and the air came.
Other times a strain would spring uncalled
As though it rose up from the shattered stones,
The shell holes and the blasted clay and bones
The barbed wire and the bombed redoubt,
Like the fairy tunes old fiddlers talked about
That came from underground and that once heard,
Notes coming from a place apart, were never lost.

After the battle, after the officer arranged the kilts
Of the dead boys with his swagger stick
Covering the genitals of the fallen;
The fishers, crofters and shipbuilders alike
Would have a swirl of notes to mourn them
And somehow fix their memories, their deaths.

The Bloody Fields Of Flanders,
The Battle Of the Somme,
The Barren Rocks Of Aden,
The Battle of Tamai,
The Heights of Casino,
All these marches, and laments for boys,
Farm lads, welders, teachers and office lads
Who never would come home,
Or if they did would often be sucked dry, fly husks
Emptied of the past, living every day
The bloody battles in their heads.

Pipe majors in their tents writing through tears
Would put down dotted crochets, minims, semi-brieves,
Filling the lines with notes that had the scent
Of heather, harness leather and the salt sea breeze.

And the streets of many a town, when those still left returned
To the bunting and the flags, would hear the skirl
And watch the brave come marching home.
Within the whirl of pride and glory the braw drones
And chanters, all the howling winds of mourning furl
And twist, winding around the rooftops, the Scots firs
The back closes, the tenements and narrow lanes,
The broom upon the hillside and the shipyard cranes.

September Sun

The soft September sun, old lady's smile,
Warms the earth, just one last time;
And back to school days, flush with memories,
Call up the blush of Indian summers past.

Something painfully beautiful yet
In this last blossoming, as though the day itself
Is wise and telling us not to fret.
'All will be well,' it says, 'All will be well.'

The Shrines

I have seen them on the Snake, the Woodhead too,
Those places where the spirits of the Earth have left.
A clutch of flowers, a soft toy, some sun-bleached cards,
A tangle of bright ribbons mark them out, these spaces now
Made holy somehow by the sudden dead.
And those behind, bereft, here mark the spot
Where love left screaming for the stars.

Here time stopped, and the smiling face
Amongst the lilies and the water jars
Is there to lay claim to this leaving place
To own this pathway to the mystery.

I have seen them too on old bog roads, a high Greek pass,
On lonely moors and Himalayan paths;
The same small sacred groves.
Some have tin houses where perhaps they think
Lost spirits live; in some an oil lamp blinks
Its flame dancing as if to call the dead souls home.

The old ones say that mourning over much
Disturbs the dead, will call them back
Causing the loved one's ghost to rise
Marooned here restless, chained by our love to Earth.

Yet still the mourners come to change the flowers
To light the tea lights in their little jars
To fix the prayer flags and make good the ground.
The mothers, sisters, friends, unconscious of the passing cars
They are the acolytes who sanctify
The earth here sensing that in some small way,
For now, for here at least, there is
Something truly sacred at this hallowed spot,
Here at this shattered wall, torn hedge, this scarred oak tree:
Their own Golgotha, their small Calvary.

One Swallow

Remember how you'd drive at night in summers past
Through fogs and mists of midges,
Blizzards of fat bugs, snowstorms of moths
All melting on the windscreen glass?
Long, hot, country miles, you'd drive
Dry eyed and squinting out into the dark, cursing,
The windscreen frosted with their last moments,
The wipers useless, washer water gone.
You'd get back home to find the hurl and heft
And spatter, the great smears of death,
The legions lost, all dashed and hurtled to their end –
Guts, brains and wings, thorax and antennae –
Pulped into a patina you'd have to soap and scour away.

But Death comes easy for them now, no battering
Oblivion at seventy miles an hour, head on,
Just the toxic rain of money slathered across
The meadows hills and downs.
One swallow makes a summer now;
Soon she'll be gone too with the bees,
The birdsong and the riotous great clamour
That once welcomed every dawn.
And, as we face each silent year
And see the dustbowl fells and fields,
We'll weep for what we all have lost:
For clouds of midges, nights alive with moths,
The scimitars of swallows, martins, swifts,
The wrens and sparrows, nightingales and jays
All the chanting birds that caroled once
All across those golden, summer days.

Such Innocence

A gun to a head, a name scrawled in a cattle truck,
And it begins again, the chimneys smoke,
The tanks roll out, men march,
And the presses bark their masters' words.
In great sweeps armies move across the map,
Towns fall to dust and borders shift.
Some time historians will write dispassionate
Long books about the siege of this,
The march of that, the bombing of there.

But, here and now, reduce all that
To a candle at a window
In a house awash with fear,
The sound of lorry tyres on cobbles,
Men jumping down, nailed boots
Come clattering across a lamplit square;
A hurried hiding of old letters, books,
And then the knocking at the doors –
With luck my friend, the door will not be yours.

The Great Un-Remembrancers

For Ken Loach and Trevor Griffiths

In a secret room off the sub sub basement
Of a lost corridor in the Ministry of Untruth,
Sit men and women with green eyeshades
Smoking, (for that is allowed here) sitting at old
Typewriters, (for nothing must be recoverable here)
Working on the Great Un-Remembrancing.

From Dingley Dell and Christmases (allowed)
Where red-cheeked uncles dance beneath
The mistletoe, and milk comes frozen home
In pails; from coaching inns where squires
Smoke their churchwardens lounged before log fires;
From all of this to where we are right now –
Where bread and circuses keep (just)
The Great Unwashed from demanding what is theirs –

The story has to somehow be expunged, arranged
Changed, twisted and rewritten so the Past
Is plastic – becomes what they decide to make it
And with all the trump cards in their hands, they fake it.

There were no riots, no Moss Side,
No Toxteth, no Black Wednesday, no selling off
Of water, gas, railways, electric, telecoms
To float the Tory boat; there was no CBI
No hedge fund billionaires, no City men to punt
The Ship Of Fools right into Chelsea Harbour.

There was only Devil Unions, unburied dead,
The Lightning Strikes the Cakes and Ale
In horny hands in the sanctum of the Devil's Den
The Yorkshireman with his pipe in Number Ten.

And the media megaphones when they're not barking of
'Celebrity Baking In The Jungle Ice Dancers'
Spew out the bile straight from the keyboards of the great
Eye shaded Un-Remembrancers.

The State, it is not Us, it is some Behemoth
Joe Stalin sent us from across the Steppes;
Society it is a vapour, Self is all.
Yet, when the Bankers took our money
To the dogs and bet on the three legged whelp,
Half-blind, that ran in circles snapping at its own blue arse,
And when the house of credit cards failed
They made us pay them bonuses and bail
Their stinking jolly boats out before they sank
The banks – too big to fail, but fail they did – ask Sid.

But before they take me to Room 101, the great
Un-Remembrancing chamber where they will
Expunge, eradicate re-make the past. I will scream out
That this is not the way things have to be,
That Everyman's long march doesn't have to lead
Us to the pit, that it is time to turn, to tell,
To shout it out, to sing, to write, to keep alive,
The phoenix that was rubble-born in 1945.

panem et circenses

On reading that ten museums were slated for closure in North Lancashire.

In Satire X of the Roman satirical poet Juvenal (c 100 AD). The Latin 'panem et circenses' (bread and circuses) referred to a Roman populace which no longer cared for political involvement. Politicians passed laws in 140 BC giving out cheap food and entertainment, 'bread and circuses' became the most effective way to keep the population from rising up in revolt.

They're closing the museums and the galleries, all
Those rooms that held small children in a thrall,
Where I stood staring at a hand-axe for an age
Imagining the caveman's horny fist gripping the blade.
The Egyptian mummy, the cruel Chinese sword,
The giant beetles and the Saxon hoard,
The Roman column and the views of how the city was;
The tins of carbide and the bobbies' lamps,
The clocking on clock, school slates, the black silk gamps,
The weavers shuttles and the coronation plates,
The stories in the cases, on the walls,
The legends and the myths that tell us all
What we were and what we are,
The Imaginarium of the raggy arsed.

They're going now: those solemn buildings made
By City Elders for the people to house our past
The People's art and craft. All going now,
The paintings and the prints,
The tapestries and pots,
Are shut away are being boxed, made ready for the off;
The libraries where books once lived
The great tools of the mind –
The tools for questioning free windows on the world
That let light in to darkness and unfurled
The carpet to the possible – so that a child somehow
Could read and dream and think.
'Oh balls to that,' they say, 'You've got the telly now.'

All gone in a blink. Ah, bread and circuses.

First they took our jobs, the work out of our hands –
Pits grassed over, steelworks – ragwort and thistle land;
Then came the food banks sprouting in the city streets;
People in their cells watching the puppetmaster's glass,
Counting their dole, listening to the hours and days crawl past.
They took our playgrounds and allotments,
Our open spaces and our common land,
And we let them, just like fools;
And then they took our hospitals and schools.

'Art and music? Books? They're luxuries
We can't afford. Get real!' We're told.
So, not content with what they'd got,
They came back for our very souls.

They are Burning the Furze

They are burning the furze,
The mountain fogged with smoke,
The stink of it, we choke on bitter ash.
Spurred on by wind, enraged,
The fire's a rabid dog, the bog
Smoulders, flickers; slick tongues of flame
Lick boulders, ancient standing stones –
For they are burning the furze.

They are burning the furze,
Settling old scores; each night
New fires burn out the vole and hare,
The hedgehog, wren, the stoat;
By peep of day smoke rolls across the bay.
And everywhere the fires,
The whole mountain ablaze –
For they are burning the furze.

They are burning the furze
And who they are
We do not – someone – knows.
The flames cross roads,
Vault mountain streams,
Leap walls, sparks spunk on roofs
Come with the west wind's helping hand –
For they are burning the furze.

They are burning the furze.
The parched hills gasp for rain,
Instead the bogs get flames.
Night comes, the stars
Are smothered, Orion gone,
And all our tiny houses wait
And listen to the manic crackle of the fire's cant –
For they are burning the furze.

They are burning the furze.
Fires flicker, sparks snicker,
The bodhran of the bogfires beats
And firestorms suck at the edges of our sleep.
The whole townland's dark dreams
Are filled with sour smoke.
And we curse them all whoever they are –
For their burning of the furze.

Bean-Sidhe

*According to Irish tradition, the banshee can only cry for
five major families: the O'Neils, the O'Briens, the
O'Connors, the O'Gradys and the Kavanaghs. My
grandparents were O'Neils.*

And I a man of sixty years, in bed
In Connemara, hears
The Bean-Sidhe scream
And I am jerked awake
The black night thick
And soft as moleskin all around
And not a light in house or out.

And again it comes: the scream,
The devil on the bog, a lost soul wails
And I am weak with tales
Told by my Dublin grandmother,
O'Neil, who heard the Bean-Sidhe twice
And lost a child each time.

I hear the howl again
And terror stalks the room,
The foul scream of a murdered child,
Doom coming from the wild
Bleak Connemara bogs.
And on it goes, the screaming
And my heart, a bloody bodhran, flogs
A rhythm you could dance a Kerry polka to.

And then? Silence. I sleep again
Fitful, cat-nap sleep, mindful still
Of something out there, something beyond.
And in the dawn's pale chill
I walk out of the house and in the rocks
Above I walk into the brassy reek of fox;

Feral and warm, metal, hot rust,
A rank sweat-stench.
Then I see my fairy woman nothing but
Foxes, a mating bitch and dog
Lust in the black night, coupling,
Howling, elemental on the bog.

The Pied Piper of Connemara

IM Martin Faherty RIP

The rat who gnawed the cable, blew the lights,
And found two-forty volts once bitten,
More than he could chew – so met his fate
And settled down to rot and stink
Between the ceiling boards and slates.

'I've no idea what brought it here.'
I told old Marty as he stopped the bargeboard hole:
Marty who had flagged the yard,
Marty who had cobbled the path,
Marty who drove the digger
And laid the drains,
Spread the topsoil,
Terraced the garden wall,
Limewashed the house,
Mowed the lawn,
Painted the doors,
Hung the gate.
Marty who could eat work and loved it with a feed
Of mackerel out the bay and a good few floury spuds.
Marty who in England built the M5 damn on his own
And could make a digger dance a jig on a tanner,
Who knocked the Severn Bridge off in his overtime
And could fix most anything with a wrench and a hammer –
Was a Free World and All Ireland authority on rats.

'Compost.' was all he said, tipping his hat back on his head,
In a way I knew would mean a telling off.
'Ye have that compost bin. That's bringin' em.'
'Ah no,' said I, 'There's nothing in it but
Old peelings, eggshells, tea leaves and crusts.'

'Eggshells!' said Marty in a voice
That scattered a hoody crow from off the roof
And sent it in a panicky clatter out across the fields.
'Eggshells! Your rat would cross the Atlantic for
An eggshell!'
          And that is why now, even though
Old Marty has gone, I smash all eggshells,
Trash them, wrap them in clingfilm
Seal them in a plastic bag and sling them in the bin,
Then put a heavy stone on top.
Not to stop the witches sailing out
In their frail, fresh-laid, corn-fed curraghs
Conjuring a storm to sink poor mariners,
But so that transatlantic rats,
Confounded, line up on the New York shore,
Not listening for the tootle of a feadóg stean
But nosing at the breeze for the Pied Piper's call
Of a large, free range eggshell hidden
Out there eastward in a Connemara midden.
They roam the New York waterfront in their millions,
Climbing to the top of the Statue of Liberty,
Deranged and dribbling, staring out
Towards something their fathers and grandfathers
Told them stories of: The Land Of Low Brasil –
With the mythical Irish eggshell in the compost heap that waits,
Golden, crunchy, toothsome, Nirvana ambrosia;
Food of the rodent gods – and just a transatlantic swim away.

Envoi – To His Feet

Well, feet, you brought me here at last,
All the way from that first wobble, what?
Some seventy-two years past?
A black and white snapshot
Finds me in a neighbor's yard across the way.
Blond and two-toothed, learning to walk,
Wearing a billy-cock hat and overalls,
I stagger with a grin, tottering towards today.

You've been at it ever since, feet;
The walking game to you has been a piece of cake –
A cake-walk you might say.
And so many thousand miles:
The Everest trail, the Hindu Kush,
The Pennine Way – no rush –
The English Lakes, the Howgills,
 Mount Brandon, the Twelve Bens, The Reeks,
The Rum Chuilinn, Slieve League,
Snow Lake to Penyghent, Keswick to K2,
All of it just a doddle to you
After that short ramble
Over Daddy Edgar's grass.

Still at it feet, seventy-two not out
And so politely too,
No push and shove, just one foot at a time,
'After you, no, after you.'
No falling out, no corns, no bunions,
Just the occasional blister caused by jealous boots,
And a frost nipped big toe, high camp, Mera Peak.

Give them a clap, hands –
Well done ankles,
Well done toes,
Well done tendons –
Quite a feat, feet.

Luath Press Limited
committed to publishing well written books worth reading

LUATH PRESS takes its name from Robert Burns, whose little collie Luath (*Gael.*, swift or nimble) tripped up Jean Armour at a wedding and gave him the chance to speak to the woman who was to be his wife and the abiding love of his life. Burns called one of 'The Twa Dogs' Luath after Cuchullin's hunting dog in Ossian's *Fingal*. Luath Press was established in 1981 in the heart of Burns country, and now resides a few steps up the road from Burns' first lodgings on Edinburgh's Royal Mile. Luath offers you distinctive writing with a hint of unexpected pleasures.

Most bookshops in the UK, the US, Canada, Australia, New Zealand and parts of Europe either carry our books in stock or can order them for you. To order direct from us, please send a £sterling cheque, postal order, international money order or your credit card details (number, address of cardholder and expiry date) to us at the address below. Please add post and packing as follows: UK – £1.00 per delivery address; overseas surface mail – £2.50 per delivery address; overseas airmail – £3.50 for the first book to each delivery address, plus £1.00 for each additional book by airmail to the same address. If your order is a gift, we will happily enclose your card or message at no extra charge.

Luath Press Limited
543/2 Castlehill
The Royal Mile
Edinburgh EH1 2ND
Scotland

Telephone: 0131 225 4326 (24 hours)
email: sales@luath.co.uk
Website: www.luath.co.uk

ILLUSTRATION: IAN KELLAS